The Prestige

East Yorkshire

John Banks

Photography by G H F Atkins

ISBN 1 898432 41 4

Front Cover Illustration -- East Yorkshire **668** (**VKH668**) was a Leyland PSUC1/1 Tiger Cub with Park Royal 39-seat front-entrance bodywork, intended for one-man-operation. It entered service in May 1957. In August 1965 it was spotted in Scarborough's Westwood bus station loading for Hunmanby on service 12A. Behind was one of the 1962 AEC Park Royal-bodied Bridgemasters which formed the link between East Yorkshire's decades of using domed-roof buses and later acquisition of standard types. **729** (**9729AT**) had a flat roof but the upper-deck windows tapered noticeably inwards. The whole question of roof outlines in the fleet was dictated by the need to run double-decked services through the arched Beverley Bar, a need that eventually disappeared when the road layout in Beverley was altered, allowing buses to enter and leave the town other than via the Bar.

Title Page Illustration -- **166** (**WF775**) was a 1927 PLSC1 Lion with Leyland front-entrance, 31-seat bodywork, acquired from Bridlington and District Motors in November 1929. It was in Bridlington in June 1935 working a town service.

>> *Opposite Page* -- Here is what caused those peculiar roof outlines. In June 1938, Brush-bodied Leyland TD4 Titan **275** (**AKH763**) negotiates Beverley Bar. Even with a domed roof it was possible to collide with the structure and it took some skill, and perhaps nerve, to drive nonchalantly through, even at walking pace. The Titan was a 52-seater dating from 1935.

Rear Cover Illustration -- A closer look, in August 1965, at the Park Royal interim design for the AEC Bridgemaster, this time on fleet number **716** (**9716AT**).

Produced for the Publishers
Venture Publications, Glossop, Derbyshire
by John Banks, Romiley, Cheshire
using computerised origination

EAST YORKSHIRE

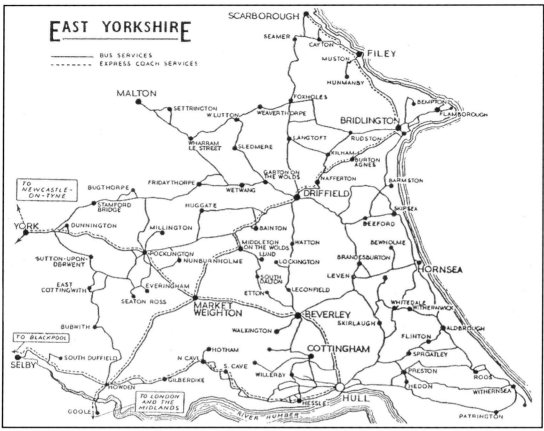

Above: The East Yorkshire territory as it stood in the early 1960s. From Hull to Scarborough was about fifty miles and Withernsea to York perhaps the same.

Below: A closer look at the area around Kingston-upon-Hull. This is from the Summer 1957 timetable.

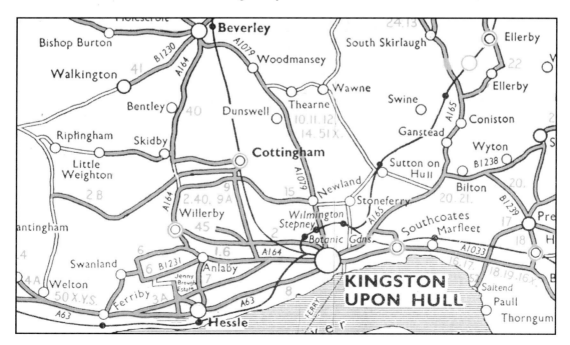

THE PHOTOGRAPHER

Geoffrey Atkins, well into his eighties and having taken transport photographs in eight consecutive decades, from 1927 to the present day, still occasionally takes a camera with him on walks in his home town of Nottingham. He was first and foremost a railway photographer, in which arcane art he sought advice and tuition from some of the great names active as the decade of the nineteen-twenties turned into the 'thirties. The techniques thus begun and developed undoubtedly influenced Geoffrey Atkins's better known bus photography.

When discussing with Geoffrey the content of earlier *"Prestige Series"* albums of his photographs, United Automobile Services Limited and East Midland Motor Services Limited, two of Geoffrey's favourite company operators, were chosen. For this, the third in the series, it was thought that East Yorkshire Motor Services Limited, as both a near neighbour of United's and another of the photographer's great favourites, was eminently suitable.

Geoffrey Atkins has never lived anywhere other than in Nottingham, the town of his birth. East Yorkshire vehicles were regular visitors to Nottingham's Huntingdon Street bus station. Scarborough and nearby resorts, in which the Company had a strong presence, were the preferred summer holiday destinations for Geoffrey and his family for many years. These locations provided a wonderful sequence of photographs of the East Yorkshire fleet from its earliest days. The Company's headquarters were in Kingston-upon-Hull. Some vehicles, particularly the flat-roofed lowbridge types, could not be seen in the coastal resorts and Geoffrey visited Hull from time to time in search of them.

Readers of earlier volumes in this series will know that Geoffrey Atkins has his own specific aim when photographing buses and coaches; as, indeed, do most transport photographers. In his case the aim is quality rather than quantity and his material is largely devoted to forming a visual record of coachwork - Geoffrey's principal interest - on public service vehicles.

In earlier decades, when there was a clear and firm separation of municipal, company and independent operators, each able to call upon the services of any one of a long list of coachbuilders now no more, bus fleets in Great Britain had a sharply defined character, a situation which lasted more or less to the end of 1968 and the coming of the National Bus Company. Municipality, BET, Tilling, large independent, small independent ... they all had their favourite coachbuilder. Occasionally the unthinkable happened, and an allegiance was changed. Some operators ordered from more than one provider of bodywork as a matter of policy ("dual-sourcing" in today's marketing jargon, "not putting all your eggs in one basket" in the homelier idiom of the era). Sometimes, too, a skilled salesman from the opposition succeeded in "getting his product in". So although there was much variety, it was contained within what was for decades recognisably a stable environment.

Geoffrey Atkins comprehensively recorded the coachwork ordered by several of the larger, mainly company, operators, from London Transport in the South to United in the North. He was not a registration-number collector. The eternal search for a picture of every vehicle ever operated by his favoured companies was not for him. The Atkins technique was to produce an image of the coachbuilder's art. If only one angle was recorded, one can be sure that it shows the product to best advantage. The vehicle recorded might have been unique or one of a large batch, but if the record produced was what was wanted, it might well remain the only one. Often though, Geoffrey took one or more additional pictures of a particular type. He recked little that they might be of the same bus. Its identity was secondary to the task of illustrating the coachwork. Locations mattered less, too. If, for example, Northway bus station in Scarborough was right for his work, Geoffrey would use it time and time again.

This might not please the seeker after multiple shots of similar vehicles in traffic scenes, in different locations and on different routes. Nor, perhaps, does Geoffrey Atkins's comparative lack of interest in the smaller independents always strike a sympathetic chord in others. That lack of interest extended to vehicles taken over from small operators, for such vehicles have undoubtedly received less attention than the standard types supplied to the larger operators. The present writer, for example, wondered about the absence of TD-class Leyland Titans among Geoffrey Atkins's excellent coverage of the pre-war London Passenger Transport Board fleet. Geoffrey explained that, although he had seen such vehicles, they never interested him: his requirements when visiting London were the standard Chiswick-designed types.

This is as it should be: Geoffrey Atkins's work is unique. He has never been profligate in his use of film. If he had been the sort of photographer who hastens round bus stations and garage premises snapping everything in sight, we should perhaps not have had his remarkable, carefully compiled visual catalogue of coachwork development over a span of sixty years from many of the most interesting operators in the country.

We complain about the gaps at our peril. There are plenty of vast collections of average, even indifferent, quality. There are no others like that of Geoffrey Atkins in which each view is carefully chosen to be exactly what is wanted. Geoffrey is not one to be put off by thunderstorms, snow, or even fog: all three can be found among his masterpieces. Despite his priority, he has occasionally turned his lens on to a traffic scene, or a general view in a bus station, perhaps to point up a contrast between the coachwork on adjacent vehicles. We are fortunate that Geoffrey has been tempted to do this relatively often with East Yorkshire. Night scenes have been a speciality, too. Not many of them, it is true, but each one a pearl. Geoffrey's cameras, lenses and enlarging equipment have invariably been carefully chosen to produce the results he personally wanted. Good equipment does not make a good photographer, but a good photographer can often be let down by inadequate equipment. Not so here. Each piece of equipment, each exposure, each print from the enlarger, is designed to produce exactly the required result. And with a remarkably consistent success rate. Few and far between have been the prints I would have liked to include, but which produced Geoffrey's gentle but firm, "I would rather you didn't use that one, I wasn't happy with it".

These pictures were not taken with publication in mind and a great many of them never have been published. This album cannot contain all of the GHFA East Yorkshire collection. As with the volume on East Midland, the emphasis has naturally fallen on what might be termed "the golden years". The pre-war material forms the splendid core, but the coverage extends to the first generation of rear-engined double-deckers and ends with East Yorkshire operating ex-London Transport Routemasters painted in the Company's original dark blue and cream livery. The vehicles have been presented - broadly - in chronological order of entry into the fleet.

One of the most pleasant aspects of the work on this series of albums has been choosing and discussing the photographs. Geoffrey Atkins welcomes me into his home, puts the kettle on, serves the tea, provides erudite comments on the technical aspects of each photograph and brings into play his formidable knowledge of coachwork as we attempt the unenviable task of deciding what to leave out. As always, my grateful thanks to Geoffrey for his patience and kindness.

I am again grateful to Philip Battersby, Ron Maybray and John D. Watson for help so tirelessly given. To paraphrase that immortal P. G. Wodehouse dedication: without their generous assistance, the book would have been finished in half the time. Ah, yes, but then I should not have been kept on the straight and narrow and had the benefit of their immense knowledge of British bus fleets and of the meticulous records they have kept over the years. If, despite their best efforts, mistakes have crept in, they are mine alone.

THE COMPANY

The writer, as a small boy, thought that half the buses anywhere in the British Isles ought to have had domed roofs. Brought up in Kingston-upon-Hull, he was daily exposed to the twin fleets of Hull Corporation and East Yorkshire Motor Services Ltd. That nearly *all* East Yorkshire double-deckers had domed roofs because of *one* low, odd-shaped bridge in *one* town of its territory, seemed not at all odd. It was odder to go to other cities and note that *none* of the buses had domed roofs.

Maturer years and an increased knowledge of geography and topography brought enlightenment. Nevertheless, it *was* possible - at least from the early post-war period onwards - to go through Beverley from either side of the town and on to East Yorkshire's destinations without passing under the Bar. We did it every Sunday in the family Ford 8 on the way to and back from York, Harrogate, Driffield, Bridlington or Scarborough. Buses serving the Market Place in the centre of town would have had to go in and come out the same way, thence picking up their route by a roundabout way through some narrow streets, but Beverley was a small town and the extra mileage would have been slight. We shall never know, now, whether building all those buses to a unique specification for thirty years from 1935 was less troublesome than altering the routes in Beverley.

The standard lowbridge types were in the fleet because of only two low bridges, one at Hornsea Mere station and the other near Selby. The latter meant that Elloughton depot was the place for a boy on a pushbike to go for a sight of lowbridge buses.

East Yorkshire Motor Services (or "EYMS", pronounced "eemz" by local schoolboys) had its origins in a 1926 British Automobile Traction takeover of two local businesses, Lee & Beulah Limited and Hull and District Motor Services Limited. Neither of those operators was very old, having begun bus operations in 1921 and 1924 respectively. The former bequeathed its sober but attractive dark-blue and pale-yellow livery to the new Company.

Although East Yorkshire went through perhaps as many changes of ownership as any other company, it managed to present an outward air of continuity and stability. There were no changes of basic livery or departures from a simple, progressive fleet numbering system, such as bedevil the student of many another operator, until the era of the National Bus

Company in the 1970s. Thomas Tilling had an interest in the Company, an interest which ensured a seamless passage to ownership by the new Tilling & British Automobile Traction Company Limited in 1928. An interest was taken by the London & North Eastern Railway in 1929. In the great split of 1942 when the Tilling and BET companies were formed, East Yorkshire followed the latter path. The LNER shareholding meant, however, that the British Transport Commission, from 1948, and later the Transport Holding Company from 1963, maintained an interest in East Yorkshire.

East Yorkshire became the property of a sole owner when the BET sold its assets to the THC in 1968, opening the way for the creation of the monumental National Bus Company, which came into being on 1st January 1969.

But as we have said, none of this was evident to enthusiast or passenger in the four decades from 1930 to 1970. The Company began with a motley collection of chassis from Leyland, Straker-Squire, Dennis and Tilling-Stevens, inherited from its two founding operators. There were a number of further acquisitions of competitors which brought ADC, AEC, Chevrolet, Crossley, Gilford, Guy, Manchester, Morris and Napier products into the fleet in small numbers. By far the best-represented chassis was Leyland. All 16 Lee & Beulah vehicles were Leylands, as were 23 acquired from Binnington's Motors Limited, of Willerby, in 1932.

Several other acquired fleets contributed examples of the Lancashire marque, and the new Company enthusiastically added new Leylands in quantity right from the start, such that East Yorkshire became to the enthusiast a "Leyland" fleet just as Hull Corporation was an "AEC" fleet. Both had a strong wartime Guy presence which did little to dispel that identification. Four decades on the writer still vividly recalls the shock felt when, at more or less the same time, Hull began to invest heavily in Leylands and the Company in AECs.

East Yorkshire and Hull Corporation had an agreement from 1934 involving the splitting up of Hull and its suburbs. Hull, unlike inland cities - unlike, indeed, riverside cities that straddle both sides of their river - is semi-circular. This 180° area was split concentrically into A, B and C. Hull claimed all money taken in fares in the A area and agreed not to operate in C. Receipts in B were shared. Most main roads out of town had both operators' buses and it was infuriating when *inward* East Yorkshire crews would not stop in the A area to pick up passengers for the city centre (or "town" as the locals had it).

Going to school involved a bus ride. The East Yorkshire Cottingham service (EYMS routes had numbers, but buses did not show them in those days) took us fairly close, but that cost a 1½d single fare. (1½d equalled about ½p.) Using the Corporation's 22 service and alighting one stop earlier where the routes diverged resulted in a saving of ½d each way. Pennies thus saved per day paid for many a bus-spotting trip to York or Bridlington. Those trips to and from school, when the extra ½d was thought worth it in inclement climatic conditions, were usually on a Roe-bodied Guy Arab or Leyland PD1. If we were saving up, the Corporation vehicle was invariably an AEC Regent with a Weymann body.

East Yorkshire tickets and ticket machines were peculiar, too. They were manufactured by Willebrew and involved the conductor in cutting off a strip down one side as far as - but not beyond or what happened to his accounting? - the amount being paid. The ticket then had to be punched to denote the stage. On a bus full of grubby schoolboys in the morning peak this is better imagined than attempted. No wonder conductors had that careworn look. Like all kids we had our stupid games. One was to ask for a "three-farthing return". We expected the conductor to know that that meant a 1½d single. Most did, but one morning I was handed three *fivepenny* returns and one shilling and threepence was demanded of me. My preferred 3d and the knowledge that I would have to walk home did little to assuage the conductress's ire. My name and address were taken and I seem to recall a well-deserved thick ear coming my way. Why *were* we such idiots? (The flat Hull accent, mumbled by a half-asleep schoolboy over the rumble of a Gardner 5LW, made confusion between *farthing* and *fivepence* easy.)

East Yorkshire's premises in Hull were as fixed as everything else about the Company. There were engineering works in the suburb of Anlaby and a vast garage closer to town on Anlaby Road. Some adjacent houses, including No. 252, housed the head office which had been in the city centre, near the railway station, until the Germans demolished it in 1941. It needs a writer a great deal more skilled than this one to describe the attraction to a schoolboy of those Anlaby Road premises. They were not particularly mysterious. They fronted the main road and almost all of the interior could be seen from the pavement outside. Journeys home from "town" on the Corporation's 69 trolleybus route passed the East Yorkshire garage, and many such journeys were cut short as a new delivery was spotted on the forecourt, leading to a hasty exit from the trolleybus and many minutes spent examining the latest double-decker or exotic coach with its "Star" name. Minutes, incidentally, which had to be answered for to a parental inquisition, the inquisitors being of that stern

EAST YORKSHIRE MOTOR SERVICES LTD

TIME TABLE

PRICE **9**^D.

Summer **1957**

2·6·57

TRAVEL BY BUS

The area agreement with the Corporation was modified more than once across the change of the decade from the nineteen-sixties to the nineteen-seventies. Worse, the National Bus Company started to paint East Yorkshire buses poppy-red and white. That took some getting used to, but there was an interesting interim period before the onset of the red when some vehicles were painted black and white with NBC logos. Geoffrey Atkins, with his photographer's eye, recalls clearly that this first NBC livery was *black*, not a very dark blue as has been claimed, and the writer's recollection supports this.

There has been much further change in the years since the

Olympian breed to whom buses meant neither more nor less than transport from A to B; who knew not a Titan from a Tiger, a Regent from a Regal, and cared less about the difference; who recked little of a small boy's wonder. Lack of parental comprehension, never mind encouragement, of their offspring's interest in buses was, and is, hard to understand, because it didn't cost them anything.

The writer moved away from Hull in April 1961, leaving behind an East Yorkshire fleet that was still instantly recognisable, despite the presence since the mid-1950s of new AECs, as that known and loved since childhood. Visits back home in the ensuing decade gave little cause for alarm - but it couldn't last.

NBC's rise and fall, including the adoption of a very fine traditional-type livery, though regrettably not the original dark blue and primrose. These later events fall outside the scope of the present work, which makes no claim to be either a fleet list or a history of East Yorkshire Motor Services. As with the earlier volumes in the series, it is a frame within which to display the cream of the G H F Atkins Collection.

John Banks, Series Editor
Romiley, Cheshire
October 1999

THE FIRST LEYLAND TITANS

Above: Ten TD1s with Leyland open-staircase bodywork came in 1929. **139 (KH7953)** was at Hull in May 1937. The vehicle behind was from the Hull Corporation fleet.

Right: Geoffrey Atkins rather disarmingly regards this shot as "a failure". It was an early attempt at panning which missed most of the bus. As a detailed portrait, however, of a two-month-old 1930 TD1 Titan and its driver it has considerable impact. **151 (KH9982)** was in Northway, Scarborough, just leaving Vine Street garage. It was on its way towards the coast and the fifty-mile run southward to Hull. The bus was new in March 1930 and this view was taken in May. There were six TD1s in the 1930 batch.

SECOND-HAND LEYLAND LIONS

Above: Leyland Lion **199** (**KH7017**) came from H. C. Motor Works (Kingston) of Hull as part of a 22-vehicle acquisition in June 1932. It was rebodied by Charles H. Roe in June 1935 and was photographed shortly afterwards in Vine Street garage, Scarborough. *Below:* From Bridlington & District in 1929 came **167** (**WF2532**), a Leyland-bodied Lion LT1 35-seater. Behind it was **219** (**WF2499**), another all-Leyland LT1, which came from Binnington's Motors Limited, of Willerby, in 1932. *>> Opposite page:* Blue Bus (Bridlington) Limited was taken over in May 1930. The sixteen buses acquired included two Leyland Lions, one of which was PLSC3 **170** (**WF1595**), seen here in Vine Street garage, Scarborough.

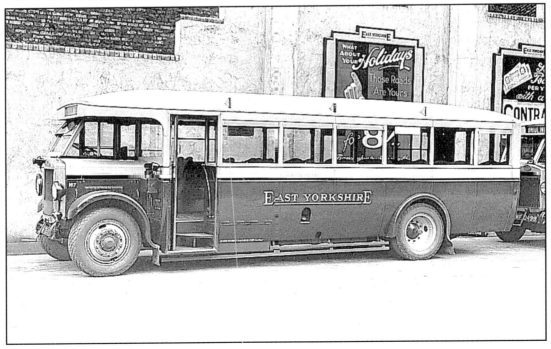

LEYLAND TIGERS

Above: **157** (**RH205**) was one of a trio of 1930 Tiger TS2 coaches for which East Yorkshire ordered Ransomes 26-seat bodywork. The photograph is an official view, taken when the vehicle was brand new, and is one of the very few pictures in Geoffrey Atkins's collection not taken by him.

Below: A scene at Huntingdon Street, Nottingham in August 1936 shows **187** (**RH4795**) on the express service from Scarborough to London. This was a 1932 delivery and was a Tiger TS4. Eastern Counties, of Lowestoft, provided the coachwork.

MORE LEYLAND TITANS

Above: The nearest we can come to an acquired Leyland Titan is this view in Hessle Square, some time after number **229** (**WF4735**), an ex-Binnington TD2, lost its original Strachans body for a replacement unit from Brush. Of the six Titans (three TD1s and three TD2s) which came from Binnington, only 229 was rebodied. The Leyland Lion PLSC3 is **79** (**WF1152**), new to the fleet in 1928. This is another picture from the collection not taken by GHFA. The print was given to him in 1935 by a friendly member of staff at Vine Street garage. *Below:* **240** (**RH8909**) was a TD3 delivered in 1934 with Brush 52-seat bodywork. It was in Hull in May 1937. East Yorkshire's offices are visible at far left of the photograph.

THE 1934 LEYLAND TS6 TIGERS

Nineteen-thirty-four's TS6s, twenty of them, came in three groups bodied by Brush, Eastern Counties and Leyland. There were eleven Brush-bodied 30-seat buses with fleet numbers 250 - 260. These are represented by **255** (**RH8924**) at Barnsley Market Place *(above)* in June 1936; and by **259** (**RH8928**) at Huntingdon Street, Nottingham *(below)* the following August. Both were on the Birmingham to Scarborough express service. The 1936 TS6 Tigers were great favourites: for once Geoffrey Atkins was not content with a single picture of a particular type, and there are several angles of all three body styles in his collection.

THE 1934 LEYLAND TS6 TIGERS

This page: The Eastern Counties version of the 1934 body was a 28-seater with coach seating. We have two views of **263** (**RH8932**), taken in May 1935 at Alfreton, when the vehicle was on its way to Birmingham. **>> Opposite page:** The photographer regards this portrait as one of his favourites. Taken at Vine Street garage, Scarborough in June 1935, **265** (**RH8934**) and **258** (**RH8927**) demonstrate how the dark lining above the cream waistrail band was extended along the autovac and bonnet side on the Eastern Counties body but not on the Brush. The vehicles have special "East Yorkshire" radiator badges in place of the standard Leyland product.

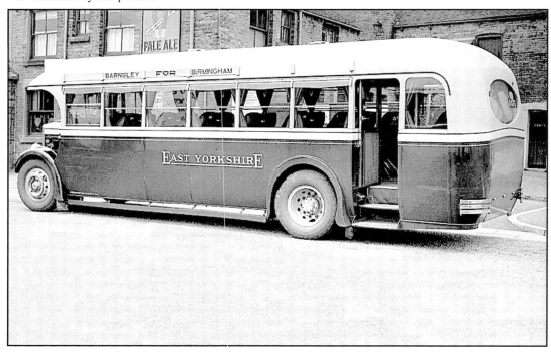

ENGLISH ELECTRIC COACHWORK - 1935

Above: Sometimes confused as Brush productions, 1935's Leyland TS7 Tigers 280 - 286 had 30-seat service bus bodies by English Electric. **286** (**AKH774**) - in the first post-war photograph to appear in this book - was at Northway, Scarborough in June 1950. *Below:* Looking very like 1934's Leyland-bodied coaches 267 - 269 *(see page 23)*, **287** (**AKH775**) had English Electric coachwork. Although it minutely resembled the Leyland product, the presence of the "English Electric" transfer on the front bulkhead, noted by the photographer, confirmed the identity. This June 1935 photograph was taken inside Vine Street garage, Scarborough.

LIVERY VARIATIONS

Above: A reversed colour arrangement for Duple-bodied 28-seater **291** (**BKH472**) at Nottingham in July 1936. The TS7 Tiger had been in service only since the previous May. 291's driver stands proudly beside his steed and incidentally demonstrates the smart turn-out that was a *sine qua non* in those days: collar and tie, uniform with shiny buttons and rather baggy trousers, cap with Company badge and summer white-top, brilliantly polished shoes. Smart those heavy serge uniforms were, but undeniably hot and uncomfortable in the summer. *Below:* TD4 Titan **294** (**BKH475**), at Cayton Bay one evening in June 1937, had no blue band along the centre of the roof.

THE 1936 LEYLAND TITANS

Above: 295 (**BKH476**) entered service in March 1936. The previous January saw Geoffrey Atkins visiting the Brush works in Loughborough where 295 was being completed for delivery. This TD4 was built with a petrol engine, soon replaced with a diesel unit.

Below: Geoffrey Atkins was very fond of the Pavilion Hotel, a noted Scarborough landmark now demolished, and wished to have this view of it included. The hotel is behind 295 (**BKH476**) in this June 1938 view of the bus in Valley Bridge Approach on its way down the coast to Hull.

THE 1936 LEYLAND TITANS

295 (**BKH476**), which the photographer had recorded under construction at the Brush works in January 1936, was caught in a stunning portrait some 2½ years later, in June 1938, inside Vine Street garage, Scarborough. By this time it had lost its petrol engine in favour of diesel power. The bus had blinds for the Hull to Scarborough service via Driffield and Bridlington. The same blind setting served for both directions as the two destinations were both on the blind. A metal flap was turned up or down as required. At the front Hull was covered (the flap was up) whilst at the side the flap was down revealing Hull as the destination. The conductor had presumably turned it before going for a tea break whilst the driver perhaps preferred to change the front flap after tea.

THE 1937 LEYLAND TIGERS

Eastern Coach Works bodied twenty-four TS7s for delivery between February and May. The first, **304** **(CKH232)**, was one of six 28-seat coaches put into service in the May. It was at Nottingham *(above)* in August 1937 on the Scarborough to London run. Representing the year's ECW 30-seat buses, **314** **(CKH242)** was one of three working a Mystery Trip Special in May 1937. The buses *(below)* were in Paragon Street, Hull outside the Company's soon-to-be-bombed offices. Six dual-purpose ECW 32-seaters included **311 (CKH239)**, seen *(>> opposite page)* inside Vine Street garage, Scarborough in June 1937 with a fine array of Yorkshire Woollen, West Yorkshire and East Midland vehicles.

THE 1938 LEYLAND TIGERS

Above: ECW supplied bodywork again in 1938. **340 (DKH448)** was a 32-seat TS8 Tiger with bus seating seen in June 1938 at Vine Street, Scarborough alongside 1936's TD4 Titan **294 (BKH475)**.

Below: Roe dual-purpose 28-seat bodywork was specified for five TS8s, 343 - 347. **345 (DKH453)** was acting as feeder to the Hull and Barnsley to London and Birmingham services in August 1938. It was at Howard Street, Nottingham. The tentative attempt at a streamlined livery was more restrained than some in the 'thirties and did not spoil too much the elegant simplicity of the Roe design.

THE 1938 LEYLAND TITANS

There were twenty-five TD5s in 1938, bodied by Brush (15) and Eastern Coach Works. **370 (ERH364)** of the ECW batch *(above)* was at Northway, Scarborough in June 1950. The domed roof, three front upper-deck windows and "stepped" frontal-profile combined to give an unusual visual effect on these buses. As, indeed, did the rebodied version *(below)*. The 1948 Eastern Coach Works design then being built in quantity on Tilling Group Bristols is immediately recognisable. Modifications for East Yorkshire's Beverley Bar usage produced a unique arrangement. **366 (ERH360)** was sitting in the sun in suburban Bridlington in July 1950.

EASTERN COACH WORKS REBODIES

In the busy Bridlington bus station scene *(above)* from June 1950 a smartly clad gentleman and his wife stroll sedately past a pair of 1938 Titans. **368 (ERH362)** had been rebodied by ECW in 1948 whilst **354 (DKH452)** retained its original Brush body. 1937's TS7 Tigers **326 (CKH254)** and **318 (CKH246)** are also visible. The houses in the background were demolished in 1983. 1939's **382 (GAT68)** was a "war baby", having entered service in December 1939. Its original Eastern Coach Works 52-seat body was replaced with a 54-seater from the same manufacturer in 1948. It was photographed *(below)* at Northway, Scarborough in June 1950.

UTILITY GUY ARABS

East Yorkshire, like many another operator, had perforce to accept chassis which were foreign to its purchasing policy during the Second World War. Twenty-two Guy Arabs appeared in the years 1943 - 1945. **404** (**GKH698**) *(above)* was bodied by Brush for entry into EYMS service in July 1943. It was at Northway, Scarborough in June 1950, as was **408** (**GRH192**) *(below)*. 408 was a December 1944 delivery and had Roe bodywork. East Yorkshire had all its wartime Guy Arabs rebodied by Roe in 1953/54. These buses, particularly after the rebodying, became a characterful part of the Hull transport scene, so much so that one was always surprised to realise that there were only 22 of them.

REBODIED UTILITY GUY ARABS

Above: A scene on the parking area, known to crews as "the muck", behind Hull's Paragon coach station (to locals it was always the "coach" station, *never* a mere "bus" station) in April 1956 includes **415** (**GRH199**) and a splendid cameo of a driver clinging precariously to the front of 1949's Titan **479** (**JAT447**) as he changes the blind.

Below: **409** (**GRH193**) as rebodied had more opening windows and more cream paint than the others illustrated, and was one of at least five thus equipped. It was at Hull on the same date as the view above.

REBODIED UTILITIES

Geoffrey Atkins has done here what we youthful bus spotters used to do by the hour in Hull's Paragon coach station. Guy Arab **408** (**GRH192**) is pulling out of the platform for the Willerby via Anlaby service *(above)*. In the next thirty seconds or so it will turn through 270 degrees and pass from left to right along Ferensway past the shops in the background. We used to watch them leave like this and then sprint the hundred yards or so to see them pass along Ferensway. There was a set of traffic lights controlling the entry into Ferensway. Perhaps 408 was caught at a red light on this occasion, allowing Geoffrey to stroll across for his second picture.

THE FIRST POSTWAR LEYLANDS

Above: The PD1 Titan appeared in the EYMS fleet in 1947. A batch of Roe-bodied 52-seaters perpetuated the Beverley Bar roof. **421** (**HAT637**) was the second of them. It was at Northway, Scarborough at 8.15 on a busy morning in July 1953. A Burlingham-bodied PS2/3 is alongside 421 on the Birmingham and London services. A later, 8ft-wide, Titan and two 1948 dual-purpose ECW-bodied Tigers are behind.

Below: 1947's single-deckers were Weymann-bodied 30-seat buses. **428** (**HAT644**) was at Wellington Street coach station, Leeds in August 1949.

MORE EARLY POST-WAR LEYLANDS

Above: The "JAT PD1s" were the epitome of East Yorkshire to the writer as a boy in Hull. They were timeless and were, indeed, still running when he left to seek his fortune in London in 1961. There were some with HAT and JRH registrations but, with the curious illogicality of youth, they were all "JATs" to us. **434 (JAT402)** was at Northway, Scarborough in June 1950...

Below: ...as was 1948's PS1 Tiger **455 (JAT423)** whose cant panels were being used for a massive sideswipe at contemporary nationalisation proposals.

THE 1948 LEYLAND TIGERS

463 (**JAT431**), with Brush 30-seat bodywork, was far from home at Derby *(above)* in September 1949 on the Birmingham service. The driver and conductor, demonstrating how and how not to wear an East Yorkshire uniform, assist passengers to descend and look on respectively. **456** (**JAT424**), a similar vehicle, was also some way outside the Company's territory at Roman Bank, Skegness *(below)* a few weeks earlier, in July 1949. It had worked in on private hire duties. 463 at Derby had a painted radiator, whereas that on 456 was chrome-plated. The vehicle looked the better for it. **>> *Opposite page:*** In July 1950 the usual frenetic scene at Wellington Street, Leeds included East Yorkshire's **456** (**JAT424**).

THE 1949 LEYLAND PD1As

Above: Pictured at Northway, Scarborough in July 1953, 1949's **486** (**JAT454**) shares the parking area with a selection of other buses including a Guy Arab which would, within months, lose its original body in favour of a new Roe unit.

Below: At Paragon coach station in September 1958 **494** (**JAT462**) awaits its next duty. The first "JATs" arrived in October 1947. 494 was one of five which came in August 1950. The registrations had been reserved as a batch and kept for three years, something that today's year-letter system would not allow.

NORTHWAY BY NIGHT

As has been evident from earlier volumes in this series, Geoffrey Atkins was a master of after-dark photography. This one was taken, during an after-dinner stroll, at 9.55 one evening in July 1953 at Northway, Scarborough. Another of the 1950 PD1A Titans, **497** (**JAT465**), was waiting to do a run to Bridlington, some twenty miles down the coast, via Cayton Bay and Filey. A West Yorkshire Bristol K was in the background with blinds for a service 43 departure to Malton. These were both late evening short workings of longer services to Hull and Bradford respectively.

UNUSUAL LEYLAND PD1As

Above: As a perfectly normal, flat-roofed, lowbridge double-decker, 1949's **505** (**JRH978**) would not have been unusual in any other fleet. The Beverley Bar syndrome made it so in the EYMS fleet. Roe built the 51-seat bodywork and the photograph was taken at Paragon coach station, Hull in September 1958. The bus had just come off "the muck", as attested by the stones in the tyre-treads.

Below: Another 1949 PD1A, **509** (**JRH982**), seen at Scarborough in July 1953, had a mercifully short-lived experimental livery of purple and primrose.

SECOND-HAND AECs

In comparison with some fleets East Yorkshire did not have a vast intake of second-hand vehicles. Those that did appear were often - like the utility Guys - at odds with normal purchasing policy. Understandable, perhaps, in the case of AEC Regal III **659** (**HWF659**) *(above)*, which was acquired with the business of Everingham Brothers, Pocklington, in November 1953; less so for another AEC Regal, **503** (**HWJ990**), one of three bought from Sheffield United Tours in 1948 *(below)*; in 1948 East Yorkshire was definitely not an "AEC fleet". 659 dated from 1950 and had a Harrington 35-seat bus body, it was at Scarborough in August 1960. 503 was a Duple-bodied 32-seat coach, photographed at Nottingham in November 1951.

LEYLAND COACHES

Above: A more predictable purchase for coaching work in 1948 was **501** (**JAT620**), a Leyland PS1 Tiger with 31-seat Eastern Coach Works bodywork, described as dual-purpose. One of three, it was at Huntingdon Street, Nottingham in August 1955.

Below: Also more in keeping was a small batch of handsome Burlingham-bodied 28-seat Leyland PS2/3 Tigers with sliding roofs, which entered the fleet in 1950. One of them, **525** (**KKH878**), features in another Huntingdon Street, Nottingham view, from June 1954, by which time it had been reseated to 32.

WIDER DOUBLE-DECKERS

The "JAT PD1s" were a hard act to follow, though their successors were doubtless purchased with other than the preferences of local bus spotters in mind. So we got the "LAT PD2s". PD2/3s, in fact, with Roe 54-seat bodies. Twenty-four of these eight-footers came in Autumn and Winter 1950. They were in truth handsome vehicles; handsomer, indeed, than the earlier 7ft. 6ins. vehicles. They were among Geoffrey Atkins's great favourites and several excellent portraits of them were committed to film. These two are of **539** (**LAT67**) at Northway, Scarborough in July 1953.

<< Opposite page: This inspired view, taken at Bridlington bus station in August 1957, juxtaposes the 8ft.-wide "LATs" with the 7ft. 6ins.-wide "JATs" (even though some of the latter had HAT or JRH registration marks). From left to right we have **543 (LAT72)**; **646 (VKH46)**, a Willowbrook-bodied AEC Regent of which more on a later page; **424 (HAT640)**; **519 (JRH992)** and **434 (JAT402)**

This page: One of the "LATs", **541 (LAT69)**, was in later years used as a left luggage office at Westwood coach station, Scarborough. Taken out of revenue-earning service in 1965, 541 commenced its new duties in January 1966. The picture above dates from July 1968. 541's predecessor was an ex-Everingham Brothers Daimler, **653 (DBT553)**, seen in the same place in August 1957.

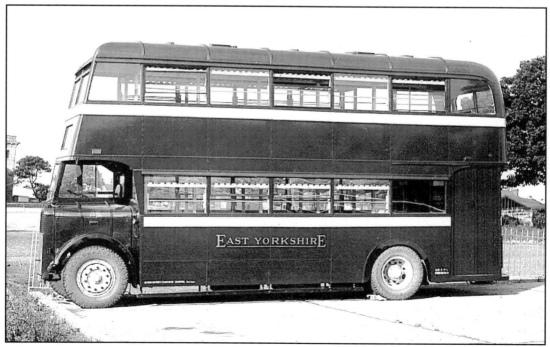

Scarborough's Valley Bridge takes traffic and pedestrians across a deep natural ravine. In some cases it has provided a jumping-off point for suicides and has thus gained a certain notoriety. Happier associations are evoked by these July 1953 views of East Yorkshire buses crossing the bridge. 1950 PD2/3 **542 (LAT70)** *(above)*, was running into Scarborough at the end of the fifty-mile journey from Hull via Bridlington and Filey. 1952 Royal Tiger **590 (MKH408)** was going the other way, towards Bridlington. These shots were taken to illustrate not only the Leylands but also various topographical details. Behind the double-decker is Oliver's Mount, a celebrated haven of walks and woods from which can be had magnificent views in all directions, especially of Scarborough and its beautiful bays. Oliver's Mount houses the town's war memorial and a network of twisty roads. In the writer's youth he often accompanied (unwillingly) his parents to motorcycle racing events there. On such days the idyllic peace was rudely shattered and the unfortunate, press-ganged youth would rather have been in the bus station armed with notebook. The ornate railings and the special gas lamps still in use at that period are also recorded.

THE SINGLE-DECK FLEET AUGMENTED

Above: Underfloor-engined vehicles appeared in 1951. **557 (LRH699)** was one of seven Leyland Royal Tigers with Brush 44-seat rear-entrance bodywork. With **445 (JAT413)** alongside it was at Northway, Scarborough in July 1953. *Below:* East Yorkshire was not alone in making use of serviceable running units from pre-war vehicles rebuilt into integral units constructed by John C. Beadle (Coachbuilders) Limited of Dartford. Leyland-Beadle **564 (LRH964)**, a 35-seat coach, entered service in March 1952 using mechanical units from pre-war TD4 Titan 301 (CKH229). It was at Huntingdon Street, Nottingham on the express service to London.

DOUBLE-DECK COACHES

Above: Perhaps the most striking (and, to us small boys, the most exciting and interesting) new East Yorkshire buses in the decade following the end of the war were the sixteen Roe-bodied 50-seat, fully fronted double-deck coaches on Leyland PD2/12 chassis. Their massive impact was rendered the more forceful because they carried the coaching livery of primrose and pale blue. **569** (**MKH78**) was at Leeds in April 1952. *Below:* When, in the mid-1950s, some of the yellow double-deckers were repainted in standard bus livery as 54-seaters they looked, to the writer at least, every bit as impressive. **582** (**MKH91**) demonstrates to good effect at Westwood bus station, Scarborough in August 1957.

MORE LOWBRIDGE AND UNDERFLOOR-ENGINED STOCK

Above: In 1951 the small lowbridge part of the fleet was augmented by the addition of six Leyland-bodied 53-seat PD2/12 Titans. The last of the batch, **589** (**MKH407**) was at Northway, Scarborough in July 1950.

Below: For its 1952 Leyland Royal Tigers East Yorkshire specified Weymann 42-seat bodies. They again had rear entrances. **596** (**MKH414**), despite its bus seats, had taken a private party to Doncaster racecourse on a glorious day in May 1952. It had been in service only since the previous March.

THE ROYAL TIGERS CONVERTED

Above: **594** (**MKH412**) in a nearside view taken to emphasise the relatively unusual use of a rear entrance on an underfloor-engined service bus. 594 was at Northway, Scarborough in July 1953.

Below: The disadvantages of the rear entrance had become more than obvious by the late-1950s and the entire batch of sixteen 1952 Royal Tigers was converted to front-entrance specification. The work was done by Charles H. Roe between 1959 and 1962. They remained 42-seaters. **599** (**MKH417**), as thus rebuilt, was at Westwood, Scarborough in August 1960.

MORE PD2 TITANS

Above: Seven PD2/12s with the expected Roe bodywork appeared in 1953. Compared with the earlier LAT-registered vehicles the most noticeable difference was a revised destination screen layout, which did away with East Yorkshire's long-standing dual-destination flap arrangement. The differences and similarities between the two batches are graphically illustrated in this July 1953 Bridlington bus station view in which **609** and **611** (**NRH220** and **222**) of the 1953 batch are contrasted with 1950's **533** (**LAT61**). *Below:* Four more Roe-bodied PD2/12s, two of them highbridge 61-seaters, came in 1955. **630** (**SRH630**) was at Paragon coach station, Hull in September 1958.

EXOTIC COACHES

Above: East Yorkshire had been fairly predictable in its chassis and body ordering for many years until, in the mid-1950s, much excitement was caused by, among other things, the start of what was to be a series of distinctive coaches. **613 (NRH654)** was a Windover-bodied Leyland Royal Tiger 35-seater with a rear entrance. In good naval fashion it was named, as "Kingston Star". It was at Midland Road, Derby in August 1955. *Below:* The lighter-weight Tiger Cub succeeded the Royal Tiger in 1954 for some Willowbrook-bodied dual-purpose 41-seaters, again with rear entrances. **621 (PAT413)** was in use on the Birmingham - Scarborough run at Nottingham in August 1954. It had been new in the previous June.

LATER LOWBRIDGES

Above: The other two 1955 PD2/12s were Roe lowbridge 56-seaters. Often seen outside Elloughton depot when the main road out of Hull went that way, **632** (**SRH632**) was there in April 1956 with 1951's Leyland-bodied 53-seater **589** (**MKH407**). The lack of a white roof and primrose waistrail on 632 made a considerable visual difference. *Below:* We didn't know it at the time, and wouldn't have believed it if told, but the 1955 SRHs were to be the last Leyland double-deckers for many a long year. From 1956 AECs were ordered. The next lowbridge buses came in 1957 and were Willowbrook-bodied Regent Vs in an even more austere livery which lacked the upper lighter band. **649** (**VKH49**) at Hull in September 1958.

BEVERLEY BAR AECs

Above: The 1956 Willowbrook-bodied 56-seat AEC Regent Vs attracted a lot of interest. All lasted into NBC days and were withdrawn between 1970 and 1972. **636** (**VKH36**) and **645** (**VKH45**) were at Bridlington bus station in September 1965. 636 had arrived from Hull via Leven on the 13D at 10.59am; 645 was passing through on service 11 from Goole to Scarborough and would depart at 11.05am. *Below:* As we have seen, the following year produced two more Willowbrook-bodied Regent Vs to lowbridge specification. A pair of 66-seaters in the same year brought a return to Roe for the bodies. This pair survived into 1972. **652** (**WAT652**) stands at Westwood bus station, Scarborough in August 1960.

STARS AND SLIDING DOORS

Above: A pair of dual-purpose 39-seat Leyland Tiger Cubs came in 1958. Despite the Park Royal bodies having front entrances there was the unusual feature of a sliding door to the driver's cab. The first of them, **672** (**VKH672**), was at Scarborough's Westwood bus station in August 1960. *Below:* The list of distinctive "Star" names for extended tour coaches was augmented with five Harrington-bodied 35-seaters on Leyland Tiger Cub chassis in 1957. "Humber", "Dales", "Wold", "Buckrose" and "Hunsley" were the additions. **675** (**WAT675**) was "Humber Star" and is seen at Nottingham in July 1958 while working an extended tour to Devon.

LEYLAND LEOPARDS

Above: East Yorkshire maintained its reputation for stylish coaches when 36ft-long chassis became available. **767 (9767RH)** was a Willowbrook 47-seater, classified as "dual-purpose". It was making good time through Woodthorpe, Nottingham in June 1964. It had entered service the month before.

Below: **738 (3738RH)** was delivered in May 1963 and was a Harrington-bodied 44-seater which carried the name "Kingston Star". The name was lost upon repainting into NBC white livery in 1973. This view of 738 was taken at Huntingdon Street, Nottingham in March 1972.

LEYLAND PANTHERS

Above: The rear-engined Panther chassis appeared in 1966 in a batch of fifteen 49-seat buses with bodywork by Marshall of Cambridge. They were impressive machines in appearance and managed a creditable 13 or 14 years of service. **803 (GAT803D)** was at Nottingham in August 1966.

Below: Metro-Cammell Topaz coachwork graced a pair of Panthers delivered in 1967. Despite being fully fledged coaches, these 44-seaters are not known to have been named in the "Star" series. They achieved NBC white livery in 1973 and were withdrawn in 1976. **823 (JRH323E)** in the same spot in April 1969.

AEC BRIDGEMASTERS

Above: The Bridgemaster replaced the Regent V double-decker in 1960. Four appeared in that year with standard Park Royal rear-entrance bodies, seating 76. It was not thought that these low-height buses would need to be of modified design for use under Beverley Bar. This quartet remained the only EYMS Bridgemasters or Renowns not to be so modified and they were soon allocated to Withernsea depot which had no Beverley Bar services. **699 (6699KH)** was at Scarborough in August 1960. *Below:* 1963's **751 (3751RH)**, at Anlaby Road depot, Hull in May of that year when brand new, demonstrates the provision of a front entrance and a return to a tapered roofline for the Park Royal-bodied Bridgemaster.

DAIMLER FLEETLINES

Above: The AEC Renown followed the Bridgemaster in 1964-66. East Yorkshire then turned to the Daimler Fleetline for double-deckers. **867 (RAT867G)** was a 1969 example. It had 78-seat Park Royal bodywork. In this September 1973 Bridlington view it was in NBC *black* and white livery.

Below: **892 (WKH892G)** was one of a batch of 1971 Alexander-bodied Daimler Fleetlines which were among the last buses to carry the original deep blue and cream colours. That livery was lost in 1975 when 892 succumbed to NBC poppy-red and white. It was at Valley Bridge, Scarborough in June 1971.

The year in which the last new Daimler Fleetlines appeared - 1971 - also saw the Leyland double-decker return to the East Yorkshire fleet in the shape of some PDR1/3 Atlanteans. The Bristol VRT and the Atlantean AN68 were prominent for some time after that. Space limitations preclude illustrations of those familiar types and we sign off this look at the East Yorkshire fleet through the lens of Geoffrey Atkins with a former London Transport AEC Routemaster.

Some time after the original livery, open rear platforms and conductors had all become things of the past for general purposes in the East Yorkshire fleet, the residents of Hull's eastern districts woke up to the familiar sight of all three, accompanied by the characteristic Routemaster sound, on the busy 56 service from the city centre to the Longhill housing estate on the edges of the city. This exercise was a product of deregulation designed to keep predators off the lucrative Longhill service. The first purchase produced seven Routemasters. Some of them entered service in a version of the original EYMS livery that lacked the white section to the roof. **804** (**WLT982**), the former London Transport RM982, was thus turned out in Ferensway, Hull in May 1988. The white roof soon appeared but photography was better without it.